My Searches For Meaning

Emily B. Scialom

Acknowledgments

My sincerest gratitude to my dear friend and ally, William Hartston, for employing his extraordinary editorial skills on this collection of poems.

Many thanks, too, to my beloved sister, Florence, for formatting the book.

Finally, my heartfelt thanks to all those who have supported me on my creative journey.

I really value all of your encouragement and assistance, thank you.

POETRY

Poetry wakes you;
It shakes you;
It's calm.
Just like a good lover
Draped coolly in your arms.
Hold these words tightly.
Almost a betrayal
Of those who hold your heart
Like Galahad and the Holy Grail.

CONTENTS:

1. GROWING UP

Poems on the passage through life.

BIRTH

The birth of another
Is something to delight in
Another story begins
On this blackened paper before us
The chaos of existence renewed

CHILDHOOD

Childhood becomes everyone;
There is no exception.
Perhaps those who take time
To learn love's foul lessons
Blossom a little later,
After unremarkable years;
But universally humanity
Has all but decreed
That childhood is sacred
And blissful
And free.

A CHILDISH SOUL

All that glitters is not gold
Say the ancients on the hill.
Yet you toil and work for more
As if the world was one great mill,
Ignoring signs for greener pastures.
God's own face creases in laughter
At your plans, your hopes, your dreams.
To conquer and own,
To beat down and overthrow,
To accumulate and possess.
No thought for your true happiness

'

AN ADULT SOUL

Far behind,
In the distant past,
Lie desires for what will never last.
Now I stand,
A mere mortal,
Yet infinite and loving;
A divine portal,
A reflection of God's vision:
His or Her or Its design.
Who knows what I could write?
Who knows what I might find
Excavating in the darkness of these
times?
Struggle and strife as bread and butter;
Everyone's full to bursting.

THE PRESENT MOMENT

Though I have been barely holding on -
Tears of confusion falling in unison -
I feel a new chapter dawning,
Though the dry skin on my hand itches
And my bones ache.
I feel I am only beginning
To know who I am.
My heart swells in writing
Of its journey to the present moment

REAP AND SOW

When you find your place in life
All seems calm, all is right.
Yet we must not plough on
Head down until the end
But be ready to adjust
Be able to bend,
For who knows what our futures hold.
Some are steeped in sadness;
Some are drenched in gold;
The reason why I certainly know:
For as we reap so must we sow

ALL MY LIFE

Holding back the suffering of my
ancestors
Even as it flows through my veins:
All the wars they fought in,
All the witchcraft they were accused of,
All the love they gave their children
Has resulted in me
Barely balancing
As if on a beam

HOLY SHIT I'M BORED

Sitting here again
Under soft light
In the home I've given my life to,
I think of summer days
In years gone past
As children running through rooms,
Giggling at uncertainty -
The opposite of how life is now.
We are serious in the face of certain
oblivion.
Cold and dark are so closely bound:
The elements are all married;
The fire's unlit;
The environment is saved.
These are the things we worry about
Now we're inside The Future
2021
Where did the time go?
What has just begun?

FLASHBACKS

When you die do you get flashbacks
Of things to regret and take pride in?
Does the tiniest moment you touched
someone's soul
As though nothing else mattered
Come back to touch you
Like the fingerprints of an angel
Upon your celestial hair?
Every experience collected together
In a film called your life.
Something certainly to treasure

WISDOM

This is it.
This is life.
You can take what you like:
A lover,
A burger,
A system,
A wife,
All is for sale.
All is free for a price,
So stuff yourself silly
With Jesus and pie.
That's the way to ensure
You'll be happy when you die
Misquoting the Saints,
Blurred in my vision,
I stumble round this confused world
On a search for more wisdom.

2. FAITH

Poems of Belief, Heaven and Angels

FAITH

Faith restores you
When things are going wrong.
It cuts like a knife
At the points of your faults;
It holds like a hand
When there's no-one around;
It keeps you alive;
Guides roots into the ground.

THINGS I DO NOT UNDERSTAND

I have never fought in a war.
I know as little of guns and bombs
As I do of spears and arrows.
I have never been to the Moon,
Couldn't point out Venus in the night's
sky,
Yet I am not without wisdom.
I have learnt to put faith in things
I do not fully understand.

BELIEVE

"Impossible!" the people cry
As the chariot arrives at the finish line.
As the bull fights back
You hear him sigh
At the archaic nature of cruelty:
"You'll never win!"
Such dreadful sin
Occupies the speakers
Of such doubt
You hear me shout
"More power to believers!"

ISLAND

"Hallelujah!" the swaying Saints cry,
Drunk on exaltation.
The first time Jesus said "I believe"
He looked just like a painting.
The world it turns in perfect harmony;
The blind lead the blind
As the visionaries wail
At the whip lashes of rejection,
As painters with their mortal hands
Attempt to paint their dreams.
I know not much of sea or land
Although I am an island.

AVALON

Avalon gleams:
It comes to me in dreams
And shadows on the wall,
The necklace I've worn
Since being given it.
A symbol of the Chalice Well
Whose origins we do not yet
understand.

RELIGION

If Jesus in his suffering
Thought he had been forsaken,
What other deeds have by mere mortals
Ultimately been mistaken?
For in His moment of victory,
Christ Himself had failed to see
The beauty of God's plan and vision.
Now He reigns forevermore,
Sitting comfortably at last in Heaven
Upon His blood-soaked throne,
Leaving no one truly alone;
Living and dying in religion's name
Is not a game:
Watch as souls fall down
A well that has no bottom,
And watch again to see how few men
ever prosper.
For Christ is the only one who has
declared His divinity
Without the accompanying din of
laughter.

REDEMPTION

Days and days
I've felt the same,
Then suddenly it's different.
Some thought provoked
A mental landscape,
Beautiful to see,
With hills and fields and mountain
ranges
Carved through by an avenue of trees
Well kept and nurtured,
Reaching high
To guide me to redemption's side

JESUS

As I travel through the desert
I am thinking of You.
In the mountains,
At the ocean's side,
I am thinking of You
More than survival.
The winds they came
The lilies of the field they blew
Everything carries a message from You

BEYOND THE SKY

Whatever lies beyond veils and skies
Is not for us to know,
For those that glimpse it are declared
Diseased and beyond hope.
In a world of blindness,
Those that see
Are shooed from place to place and
need
A helping hand to steady them
Before they fall and don't get back up
again.
I've read their depictions with curiosity
Of a divine presence and angels
gathered,
All with gifts around them scattered.
Understanding, vision, clarity
Who wouldn't hope for that?
I know that others wish to be
In the realm of knowledge,
Far from the mournful cries of the
ignorant.

THE KINGDOM ABOVE

Jesus watches over me,
Come rain or come shine.
His are the hands which are holding me
Above all waterlines.
I pray to God to embolden me,
To carve these declarations of love.
I recognise few things around me
That compare to the Kingdom above.

GHOSTS

Now I see you;
Now I don't.
Then we hear you;
Soon we won't.
A spook, a fright,
A terrible break in reality's schedule,
Who are you?
"Go back to the light!"
I say, standing trembling,
Deep in life's pitch black night.
Then I see you standing there,
Flicking back your gentle hair
From a face, evil so fair.
With you I'd sway in rocking chairs.

FALSE GODS

Another tomorrow is in my hands -
How many more to go?
The fortune teller speaks to the kings
and the homeless
Saying "Wouldn't you like to know?"
As the beasts go in for supper
And the snakes, they take their place
At the awkward banquet of life;
Who'll be denied God's fair grace?
It's not for us to judge
Or argue amongst ourselves
Who will ascend into Heaven,
Or else, in defeat, go to Hell,
But rather we must do our best
In the face of daunting odds;
For narrow is the road to redemption
And many are the false Gods

HEAVEN IS MINE

Whether I make it or not
It's interesting to watch
The fall, the climb -
Eternity's mine
As Jesus told me it would be
And through my faith,
Infinite hearts I could touch.
Heaven is mine already.

POSITIVITY

We're due some positivity.
So much stress, so much strife,
So much negativity,
Don't you understand life?
You get what you give,
So give your all to God
For He or She has the answers
That others do not.

3. LOVE

Poems of Love and Other Virtues

LOVE

Love has its charms:
Its pain and its harm
Strike you in the night
And caress you during the day,
Until all at once
Like a natural disaster,
Love goes away
To hold another hand,
To brighten another's world
And you yourself are wistful
With so much to give.

APHRODITE

It cut me off;
It stirs my veins;
It's the pulse in my heart.
Let's start again.

Lifetime after lifetime
We must persist
With the righteousness of virtue
To feel the bliss of the Goddess's kiss

She shakes me up;
She must not stare
Through flesh and bone
And spirit and air.

Millennia after millennia,
Past the realms of time,
The Goddess whispers again:
"I'll make you mine..."

Until all must submit
Each hand, each thought,
To the divine source of true beauty:
The Goddess of Love

PEACE

Despite the chaos of all eternity
I feel a dawning sense of peace.
Priceless, it's been found:
A way to cease the whirling dervish
Of my mind and its desires
Of my body in its frailness,
Of my soul in all its wildness.
Finally I've found peace.

SHALOM

Shalom is a holy word
Steeped in ancient ritual.
It was there in the time of the Pharisees
It will be there at the end of all Earthly
things
Bestowing blessings on all its recipients
Engendering trust where perhaps there
should be none

A STAR IS BORN

A star is born.
Do you feel my light
Burning brightly
In life's night?
Each word I write
Is as each breath I take:
It teaches me about my fate.
Two stars collided:
Oh, the mess
Created by true happiness,
Now long ago.
I burn alone,
Provocative in my golden glow.
But true love's touch
Awaits me still.

ALWAYS

Working towards golden horizons
I toil, bleed, slumber.
Slow progress,
But your love lights the way,
Supporting me each step of the journey.
You flinch at their laughter.
My triumph is your triumph
For we are connected
Through time and space.
Always.

LOVE AGAIN

To express your love is such a gift;
Not many find the words for this.
Too busy caught in the mindless
maelstrom,
Torn asunder from their true selves
At such a young age,
Such an early stage;
Told not to cry,
To keep it all inside,
Until one day it comes screaming out
In alcoholic rages.
Genetically impaired,
A murder victim at your own hands.
Not for me the life of unexpressed
emotion:
In breathing I feel the urge to create,
I suck in respect and breathe out pure
intentions
For a better tomorrow.

ONE LOVE!

One love!
Don't you love to hear it?
Wouldn't you love to see it?
Do you even believe it?
Do you need to be it?
Repeat ad infinitum
Until it's been achieved,
Powered by the lungs
Which God has given me.
Digging for treasure in my soul.
This is what happens
When immaturity grows old

LOVE IS A GOOD THING

I have to hibernate to get away from
most things:
The people; the wind;
The nonsense; the din;
The wastefulness; the sin;
The hungry; the starving;
The freezing; the hardening
Of time as it scuttles down the back
streets
Of your mind.
Reminiscing of good things and all the
dreams gone past.
We say as we eat our way through the
supplies:
"Good things never last and true love
never dies!"

4. RELATIONSHIPS

Their joy and sadness

INSIDE MY HEAD

Pain.
I'm in pain.
How do you rhyme that?
With "rain" like a thunderstorm.
They're never coming back.
All the years I wasted:
Unfocused dreams
Sliding through my fingers again and
again.
I just need a friend
Who'll laugh at my jokes.
My existence,
Which is barely hanging from a thread,
Inside my head.

TO FIND YOU

This is the frontier of creation:
All previous choices have led us here
To this moment.
I embrace you with my thoughts,
Chaotic yet free.
I care enough to live a miserable life
But not so much it drowns me.
Flying high above the problems and the
lies
I let the jokers and the clowns be:
I don't want to know them,
Or for them to crown me;
A part of their kingdom I will never be.
Mine is a serious world;
Won't you brighten it & join me?
Bring a smile and a good joke,
I don't want you to bore me,
Tease me then torment me
And finally ignore me.
That's what I'm used to
In this world that men built.
I offer bricks of compassion
I wish to watch as passion and trust
Combine like true partners.
Find you I must.

FAMILY

When all the cruelty's said and done,
When evil's had its way,
There still will be a handful of people
Who'd give you the time of day.
In the right circumstances,
When looked at in a certain light,
This is a gift of such beauty
It shatters my hatred of life

HOME

What have I found in my quest for life?
Confusion abounds,
Along with struggles and strife.
Our true nature abandoned:
Her hands have been tied
To stop her from searching
Each day and each night.
For better connection,
Love, even alone,
Someone to go searching
When you don't come home

I LOVE YOU

There are not words to communicate
That which I feel for you.
I took such pride in your every breath;
You know I believed in you,
A mental warrior, a bloody heroine, an
artist of some stature,
You couldn't draw one scene of
redemption
In your extensive collection?
The tragedy of wasted talent
Has stayed with me through the years
If only to see one more scribble
That could bring the cold-hearted to
tears

TO BE LET DOWN

To be let down is bad enough,
To be abandoned or betrayed,
But to experience all three at once
Is too much to ask in a single day.
Thus it was many years ago
When my life was torn asunder;
Even in talking about it now
I feel that fateful thunder
Of my inner storm:
A child is born
Only to be forsaken!
On anniversaries the ceremonial torture
Means my heart it still is breaking.
One day I'll be at peace again,
As on the first day I slept
But until then my pillow is drenched,
For years and years I've wept.
I wonder where you are right now
Where you have been all these years.
The toil and stress and hurt are mine
Now you are no longer here.

NO ENEMIES, PLEASE

On the great battlefield of life
I am unarmed.
I seek not to hurt you;
I mean you no harm.
In truth I am much closer to
Wrapping my broken arms around you,
Blood pouring down,
Just like my tears.
Yet we've made enemies of our souls.

IN MEMORY OF YOU

Friendships come and friendships go.
Into the wind they blow
To be held by another hand,
Far away in distant lands

Though I sometimes think of you,
All along we always knew
You don't see me, bright and true
Like I see you, scarred and bruised

Now we're on different plains,
Never to return again
To the nights we laughed at tragedy.
Being with people who weren't meant for
us.

Into the realm of trust I glide
Far away from view
Though the thorns prick at my side
In memory of you

FOR YOU

You go deep into my world of pain
Looking directly at the wounds.
You flinch, not to see reality's stare
Watching from across the room.
Your bravery becomes you.
I stand in awe
At what I see before me:
A kind heart is a sacred door

FOUND SOMETHING = YOU

Who knows what I might find?
Which grave I'll plunder,
Whose stairs I'll climb.
Memories of you flood my mind,
Years before the dawn of time.
There laid a you and a me
In blissful serenity.

YOU GET ME THROUGH

One and a half million dead;
The virus still not done.
The vaccine can't come fast enough:
It will still be rejected by some.
A suicidal planet surrounds me.
What am I going to do?
Keep on living and laughing,
Always loving you.

STONES CONTAIN JEWELS

I'm still in shock
From the day I lost you,
The day you stopped the clock
In the procession of time.
Redemption is mine
When this shame can be forgiven:
Within you,
Without you,
And all about you.
The answer, always, is love;
But the day all this pain
Turns into rain
And showers upon the desert
Is a day so fine
It makes Dali of my mind.
A painter depicting a scene
Of melting time.
These words of mine
Find jewels in the dullest of stones

WEIRDO

I can't be what you want me to be:
I never have conformed
To school or band or writing collective;
I have not signed up to be part of the
norm -
It's out of my pay bracket.
It's not my cup of tea.
I'm too busy counting stars:
One for you;
One for me.

I'M WAITING

I haven't truly left your bed
Since the moment you left me.
Part of me is still waiting for you
To take back your words.
Here I lie,
Capsized,
Wishing that we had never started.
Jesus showed me love;
You showed me disaster.
All are lessons learnt through pain.

FOR WHAT IT'S WORTH

One minute I write for you;
The next there's another.
Once I'd have lived and died for you;
Now I love you like a brother.
In the extended family of planet Earth,
I'll love you always for what it's worth.

REGRET

Regret will not be the death of me
Though it is so real.
It almost breathes.
Replayed moments
Now have scratch marks and
distortions.
Dream and reality collide sometimes.
But I didn't know the importance of word
nor deed
And what a mess I made.
I'll be picking up the pieces forever.
But that's okay,
Because for just a moment I knew that
love is real.
Far beyond these scoundrels,
Way over those far flung hills,
There you lie
Untouched by time.
I visit you more often than I care to
admit,
Each thought of you a blessing I sadly
kiss

TRUST

Trust is not easy to come by:
It's earned; it's there; it's gone.
If you've lost your faith in people's word
The end will not be long.
Love and music heal the wounds,
But sometimes that which can't be
regained
Is worth much more than gems and
gold:
The absence of all games.

I HEAL

The blank page judges me
Says "what have you got?"
And I must show it day after day
I'm not something I'm not.
Proof with all certainty that something is
at last right,
A writer who is writing through darkness
into light.
Clarity will be mine
One day before I rot
And disintegrate into darkness
That is the human lot,
But not mine alone to bear.
I at least have company:
You'll hold my hand
You'll bring me hot chocolate
And witness my almighty scream
Through day and night
I don't know how you tolerate it
Seeing someone so nakedly real
The desperation, the strife,
Nothing will suffice
Until one day I heal.

THE WINDS THAT BE

These words reach you on angel wings:
The halos of the well intentioned
Adorn their crowns.
You know I have found
A way to make you smile
The way you used to when you were
young,
Unafraid of what you would become.
Unconscious almost,
Running free,
Before we were all lost in a storm of the
winds that be

DEAD STILL, NOT MOVING

Tearing through the darkness,
I find you lying there,
Six feet under Earth's surface
Yet gasping for air.
I dig and dig and dig
Until you return to me,
Until we are free
Of the mistakes which made us
crumble.
In this global dark night of the soul
I fumble
For the words to make you real again.
Let's go back to when we were both
sane

JUST LOOK AT YOU

I feel like writing every time I look at you.
There's something about your eyes
Which makes me think of the deepest
ocean's blue;
There's something about your smile
Which teaches me everything I need to
know
About your despair and your mother
And how I can meet you there;
There's something about your hatred
Which is so similar to my own:
The music that's just not good enough,
The people you've outgrown.
There's something about your hair
That shines as a Temple, gold
To enshrine the mind you worship God
with;
Why doesn't it grey as you grow old?
There's something about the hope you
hold for the future
And how it's infectious when you're with
me.
Today, tomorrow and maybe the next
day
I now wish to see,
And though we may be haunted,
We are still as real as sin.
Betrayed from all sides like we are
We must now reach within.
So come with me for treasures dear,
Who knows what we might find?
But one fair jewel I see, so clear,

Was the day that you became mine.
"We must not part,
We must not feel sorrow,
As long as we have each other!"
We are but crowns and rings
Worn by another and another.

BROKEN IN THE POST

Everyone's a vulnerable person
nowadays,
We're all fragile as Hell.
I arrive at your doorstep
As if broken in the post.
You let me in anyway.
You're kinder than most,
Accepting faulty goods
Because you know
We all have our faults.
That's how we grow.
We're all moving towards the light of
love;
That much is assured.
We rage against our mortal
imprisonment
As the wave attacks the shore.

RIGHTEOUS ROMANTIC

We all make mistakes:
People let go;
Hearts they break.
Fast forward several lifetimes,
You know what I see?
The same soul in the morning
Staring back at me.
For we will meet again
Until we get things right.

ALL THE WAY FROM HEAVEN

If I were to leave you standing there,
Freezing and blue,
How cold would you grow without me
beside you?
For nothing has compared to that which
I felt
When you left me in life's snow:
A motherless existence.
Nothing can compare.
It'll break your back -
You must have heard the snap,
All the way from Heaven,
And my screaming in despair.
Have you since met me there?
You thought you didn't matter;
I want you to know the truth:
In all my long days and longer hours
No one mattered more than you.

LANDSLIDE

Emotions overwhelm me,
Expectations to drown in.
Missing your presence,
Mourning the memories
While trying to think of the future.
So blurry, so surreal,
I feel drunk in my soul

WORDS THAT BRING PEACE

I've created a dove
With only words
That brings me peace.
Just like the bird,
When I am lonely
Words are there
To bring me tea
And stroke my hair.
They're always soft
Just like my heart
It sure is hard
Being this far apart.

TO FIND YOU (II)

To find you would be a storm in a quiet
sea.
I'm sure we would find treasure in
surviving
To teach us of our mortality,
And which to reach for among your
hopes and dreams
At the point your struggles turn to
screams.
To hold you would be a ray of sunlight,
Caressing a tulip in full bloom;
To know you would be the stars of
Heaven
Arranging in my name;
To love you more than any other
The universe must break,
For love can touch more than once in a
lifetime.
Like a bad guest it comes and never
leaves
But stays there beside you;
If not deep inside you,
A blur of infinite bliss
To treat you right
Would be a credit to my mother and
father
And all the mistakes I've learnt from.
To have you here, always near
I am preparing for my heart to be your
home

5. TRIUMPH and DISASTER

Hopes fulfilled and disappointments
suffered.

TRUTH

Chasing happiness
Down the side streets of my soul,
Eking out a smile
From a bottomless well,
Joy will be mine,
I can just tell.
You can't ignore the miracles
Which grace each of our lives;
I give thanks to that which lies behind
them.
It's not a cruel lie.
Truth I've found:
I share it freely
With all who listen,
Anyone who sees me
Beyond the flesh,
To my inner purpose:
Shining like a diamond in the mud.

GREATNESS

Day turns to night
Like struggle and strife turn to wisdom.
I have so much to tell you, child,
If only you would listen.
I was there at Hastings;
I put hand prints on caves in France;
I know all about bows and arrows;
And love,
If you will give me a chance.
The day that I gazed upon Greatness
I wanted to know his soul.
I hope that he'll feel similarly,
And together we'll grow old.

HOPE

Hope sneaks up on you
As the days pass.
Perhaps I will find happiness at last
As self-awareness grows.
What brings gifts,
What brings strife,
Begins to be brought
From shadow to light

THE SEASONS QUICKLY TURN

Don't you get it?
My success is your success:
If I stumble, you will fall.
We are but one being,
Karma rules us all.
Getting what we give,
Receiving what is ours.
In this lifetime,
In ten lifetimes,
The seasons turning like the hours.

VICTORIOUS

The pandemic has brought loneliness,
Death and despair.
But as long as you're still standing,
Breathing in and out
You are victorious.
The world has surrendered;
Nature does rule
Over the meek and the mighty,
The poet and the fool

DESPAIR

At the bottom of a cliff
You will find me there,
Crumpled and broken
A child fully grown
Looking for somewhere to call a safe
home.

One can struggle and toil
To start life anew,
But when you find faith
The fortunate will laugh at you.

I'm already broken;
There's no harm can be done.
You will think me crazy
While I will think you numb

A BIBLICAL POEM

Another line for another poem:
You aim for the Biblical and get the
absurd,
What has become of my future, my
world?
Shut up and wasted
Each day and each night.
Waiting for a vaccine
Like a man for his wife

THOUGHTS

I know who I am,
But the world doesn't recognise me
Though I've been here many times,
Reforming like the waves of the sea.
I come now in the form of a woman from
England,
Scribbling furiously onto a page,
Through trial and torment,
overwhelmed.
Creation must still rage,
Like screaming children, never quiet,
I always have something to say:
Like Pluto was, then wasn't, a planet.
My good mood turns from night into day:
An empath's smile, soft and tender,
Will surely grace my face
The day you tell your sorrowful story,
With sincerity that can't be faked.
Every man, woman and child
Partakes in the human race.
We are all to be held responsible
For our collective fate.
Into the unknown we feel ourselves
plummet.
So do your best despite the odds
You will reach the mountain's summit.
Ignore the laughter of the gods,
The juvenile rulers of everything,
Measuring out fortunes with clandestine
whims.
A hopelessness dawns on me, deep in
my soul;

I watch as all around the future grows
old

MORTAL

Flesh and bones,
That's all you are -
Though you can spell
And play guitar.
A rock star you will never be;
A writer maybe;
We shall see.
So carve and plunder,
Toil in drizzle,
For you might find something
Worth searching for.

HISTORY

Fact and fiction intermingle
When history is spoken.
Who can say, who was not there?
What heart or promise was broken?
What sky was touched?
What stars were plucked?
What marathon ribbon torn?
If all is recorded by the calculated
winner
And the well-intentioned loser is forlorn.

DREAMS ARE DRUGS

Dreams are like drugs:
Make them illegal.
"There's nothing to see here"
Except the remnants of thoughts,
Some very far flung.
The visions for tomorrows yet to pass

DREAMER

Dream away!
You know it's safe
From flashes of meaning.
You can create
A world worth being in:
Characters and storylines
Approach on the horizon;
You grab them fast
For you know they contain
A hole that you can hide in.
In the white heat of the battle for eternal
life,
Deep within you there's a calling
To make a better world

FRUSTRATION

I want to be so many things
I have many hopes, much to dream
I want four arms and seven legs
To walk and do all of my chores
Two heads
To share the worry
One dream to work towards
I want to be an astronaut
So I can touch the stars
Yet I also envy Earthworms
Protected by the dark
I don't want to wish my life away
Never achieving anything
But can one be completely normal
And also view the Gates of Heaven?

FAME

To introduce dream to reality
You first must believe
In the forces which drive us,
The powers that be.
Some have a vision
Beyond what is acceptable;
Others have dreams
Which are ultimately unfaithful,
Shared commonly,
Like a virus
The desire for fame.

CROWNED AND ANOINTED

Fame is for the broken-hearted:
People without love,
Trying to mend themselves visibly.
Through acceptance we can be free?
If only it was so simple:
As the bars rise from the ground
The rose pricks the holder.
There's blood coming from your crown.
The stable boy sits crying
In an empty stall of peace;
There are people at the windows
Trying to gain an evil peek;
There's footsteps of doubt in the corridor
Though no one ventures there;
There's a scream inside your mirror
And one cannot help but stare.

THE DEATH OF BEAUTY

Overwhelming feelings;
The dam bursts to a flood.
At this point I am thinking
When will there be blood?
Failures on so many levels,
The lost pretend they're found,
As beauty bows her aging head
And crawls under the ground

STOP

Everything and everyone is falling apart.
I want to make it better
But I don't know where to start:
The polar caps are melting;
I hear monkeys screaming;
As our primal selves
They cry clean through the evening;
I don't know where we're going
anymore.
I want to press STOP
But we're falling off a cliff
And I just can't get off

I'D FOLLOW ME

Unfollow me, follow me,
Block me, don't reply.
See if I care
As the day turns to night.
Each day that passes, my wounds turn
to wisdom,
Yet I can barely tolerate this world and
all its rejection.
I'd follow me:
I know my heart's good;
My intention's impeccable;
I'm not a tree in a wood -
I'm an angel in McDonalds,
A tear in the desert,
A cry in life's pitch black silent night.
I am searching for my root source.

A PRAYER FOR THE DISENCHANTED

When I was younger,
Nothing but a child, it seems,
Night after night I prayed to be
The most beautiful woman in the world,
Inside and out.
Now I am grown
And I'm tired of my dreams.
My body's exhausted,
My soul's torn at the seams

THE ISLE OF DREAMS

Hit me with the truth:
Hard, no flinching.
I want to know what's real so badly
I've been pinching
Myself all the time
Since my dream awakened
And then turned to pieces,
As my heart was breaking.
When dreams turn to dust
You must throw them to the wind
On a sacred isle.

CHRISTMAS 2020

I hope to salvage some festive cheer
From down the back of the sofa.
I know it only happens once a year,
You know I don't pray that it's over,
But this year it's so different:
We all feel alone
When we should be together.
The old ways have been overthrown

POET, PLEASE WAKE ME FROM THIS NIGHTMARE

Aren't you the poet?
Shining light into the darkness
With a candle of warm words,
Bringing smiles to far off lands.
I guess they've all heard
Your cry by now.
I'm wondering how
We'll ever get out of this storm.
There's chaos in creation,
There's never quietness
In the mind of a creator.
Noise and bustle,
Another dream on the hustle
Jostling for presence
In the infinity of consciousness.

OVERCOME

Each step I take,
Each breath I breathe,
Must lead to something.
Don't you believe?
Heaven and Hell,
I know them both well.
The people have bickered
About their Gods eternal
For forever until now:
What is real?
You can feel somewhere, somehow
That something's not right.
For the future we must fight
And come together as one
In order to overcome.

HOPE (REVISITED)

Hope is a word with a bad reputation.
Put in the corner, ignored, unheeded,
It's broken many hearts,
Destroyed lives at times.
Drowning in delusion
The hopeful march off cliffs like
lemmings.
Yet when hope sees reality from across
the room
And they start to dance,
New life can be born.

LIBERATED, AT LAST

Liberated
While stuck between the same four
walls;
Hibernation in the land of the free.
Who could have anticipated?
Who could have foreseen?
A leaning towards the light of
self-betterment
Turned into a trip too close to the sun.
Turn around! Turn around!
The pilot won't.
The trouble has just begun.
Ignoring nature?
A stampede.
Adoring God?
A trickle.
These are the materials I work with;
This is my palette for greatness.

6. DOUBTS

About people, the world and the future

DREAM AND/OR NIGHTMARE

I'm living in a dreamland
Which few have dared envisage,
With food and love aplenty.
I'd love for you to visit.
I'm living in a nightmare
Which cannot be described;
It goes beyond all realms yet ventured
By the poets and the scribes.

BORED NOW

Racism?
Yawn
Sexism?
Yawn
Homophobia?
Yawn
Transphobia?
Yawn
Political rivalries?
Yawn
War and bribery?
Yawn
When did the world get so boring?

A BLEEDING HEART

A world of pain and strife,
Just to get through life.
How are we to succeed
When always on our knees?
Through economic hardship,
Or by weight of memories,
The back now becomes crumpled;
The heart begins to bleed.

NIHILISM

If all is meaningless then why write
these words?
Why try to connect beyond borders,
beyond taste and opinion, beyond
even life and death?
If all is meaningless let's all kill
ourselves
And find out for real the truth about Hell
No, I say nothing is meaningless,
Though we are free
To bestow meaning or not upon lyrical
gifts from me

RACISTS

I would go so far as to say
Racists are unevolved beings
Stuck in tribal times
With no way of seeing
Which way is up and which way is
down,
Even as they fall to the ground
From a great height of ignorance.
Those times are over;
Those days are gone.
Now is the time for us to become one
And unify together,
Through the pain and strife
As if each man and woman on Earth
Is as dear to you as your husband or
wife

I AM NOT A RACIST

I am not a racist,
A sexist,
A fool,
I'm proud of who I've become.
When I saw the wild eyes of prejudice in
the darkness
I knew that I had to run
Far from the thinking that consumes
these hounds.
Lord help us when they smell the blood
of innocents.
They know nothing of love or oneness,
Nothing of the sort can they
comprehend.
It's always "mine" and "theirs" or "us"
and "them",
Who do they call on when they need a
good friend?
They only know shadows, hatred and
greed.
I'm thankful I'm thoughtful, faithful and
free

BREXIT

To what do we owe this honour?
"To the people!" they do cry.
Freedom, control, a world beating
vision,
Let's move towards it
For the children.
To give them
Hope, autonomy, a functioning
economy.
But the children go starving
As politicians count their dough

NOT MUCH OF A PRIME MINISTER

I wouldn't trust Boris Johnson with a
fiver,
Let alone to control a nation
At war with itself on many levels.
He has ideas above his station,
Praying the Britain of the past
Will let down her golden hair
To climb to her despite impossible odds.
We're living in a Dreamland,
Quickly transitioning into a freeloading
nightmare.
Money to your mates,
While the children go starving
Needing aid from UNICEF
Just to meet the margins.
The destitute, the despairing,
We all will meet you there,
In a place of not knowing
A future we can bear.

AMERICA

At least we're not America.
The statement echoes around the world
As kids in cages gather.
Little boys, little girls,
Desperate for a better life,
They're at the border day and night
As riots in the streets persist.
To make the message clear,
Racism's day is over.
A new world enters here
As guns in children's hands are placed
As your chief lunatic
Pours hatred into microphones
Inspiring the depraved
To burgle decency's home.
The redwoods are burning,
Paradise turned to dust.
But in any way we can
Help you we must,
To find clarity of vision,
Be as one with each other.
For in black and white
We have sisters and brothers

I DISAGREE FOR ALL TO SEE

What's going on with America?
Free guns with every Big Mac;
Racism in place of justice;
You're moved to the top of the first class
If you express solidarity with a flag -
A dream and an image combined.
Riots in the streets;
Distress for all to see;
The homeless by the redwoods;
The empty chairs at dinner time.
They're still searching for gold
And yearning for slaves.
Those slaves' ancestors
Now have houses in the Hills.
The changes are hard to keep up with:
Socialism scares you,
Policed by your own thoughts
Taught to you in childhood
About those who belong
And those who should merely sing
songs
In the cotton fields.
I disagree for all to see.

NEW DAWN

All the stars are falling
From the American and European flags.
Divided we'll be conquered
By hopelessness and tabloid rags
As poverty hits the millions.
The tidal waves are due
As Mother Nature raises her voice:
Is the problem you?
With your consumption and
competitions
All must be renewed;
This troubled planet must find focus
In its blur of green and blue:
The green being redemption
Ever present here,
The blue being destruction
Some will love to hear.
But all the while each flower, each child
Reaches for the light.
It's adults who face the consequences
Of turning day to night.
Which stage are we in now?
A new dawn must be near,
A dream to carry us over the mountains
Of peril and real fear.

POPULARITY

Popularity is not the answer.
You can toil and slave
At the coal face of opinion
All day and all night,
Yet wake up at dawn a hated man.
You can have everyone in the room love
you for who you are,
But if you don't love yourself
You're wasting your time.
"I'm looking for approval from others"
"I am watching the rain fall outside my
window."

ILLER THAN THE EARTH

Sick poetry,
Take me to the hospital.
I'm iller than your grandmother
After a rollercoaster.
Rolling ciggies in festival mud
While watching Kate Tempest at
Glastonbury, my love
Like Isaac Newton under an apple tree.
I did hear a thud ring clear:
The Chief Spirit communed with me,
Told me I'd a writer be.
Now I'm focused like no other
Iller than the Earth.

DREAM

If I had an idea,
I'd share it with you;
But the fact of the matter is:
I don't have a clue.
What tomorrow will bring
And what the future will hold
Are fodder for the rich,
The white and the old.
We, the people, are passengers
On a sinking ship.
Try as we might,
We can't end the fight
Between the haves and the have nots,
The blacks and the whites,
The weak and the noble,
The spark and the flood.
All is at war,
Or so it would seem,
As images of the past come to me
As if from a dream.

SAVAGES

I'm tired of the fear
Of death and disease,
Of the guilt for leaving a light on,
Of being part of the problem.
Pigs in blankets,
Why don't you eat me?
It's just as savage.

ABORTION

"Abortion is a human right" -
Watch as the women like cats fight
For their voices to meet the
microphones
To capture their despair at being
overthrown
In the great fight for survival.
It's not a man's world:
This world belongs to everyone, little
girl,
So listen when mama's speaking.
Ask questions, make her talk
About the lost generations
And the lack of change.

NO LONGER CAN WE STAND IT

There's a huge problem.
Ask the girls who have had their genitals
mutilated;
Ask the women denied an education.
It's called gender imbalance.
I know that you haven't thought about it
enough.
The roots go deep,
In Church, in state,
Dictating marginalisation as a woman's
fate.
No longer can we stand it.
Raised words as raised swords,
We'll fight against this cruel world
Filled with cowards who call themselves
heroes.

EVERYTHING'S FOR SALE

Broccoli's cheap;
Diamonds are expensive.
Broccoli helps you live;
Diamonds are to die for.
Money is the root of all evil,
So they say
As they rattle their jewellery.

UNITY

When day turns to night,
As we watch the light go
We all feel sorrow
For our time in the sun.
The end has begun,
A new day must dawn,
But it takes so long.
The battles rage on
Between religions, colours, nations,
creeds.
With all this division
How can unity breathe?
It lies dead on the battlefield,
A theory at most,
The looming towers of Justice
Exhibiting strange smoke.

ANOTHER MISUNDERSTANDING

No one understands the poets:
They speak in rhymes and riddles;
They don't do the washing up;
They can't meet you in the middle.
A normal life and a poetic life
Are not the same thing.
You don't understand.
A true genius is a bird born with
oversized wings,
Free to go where others cannot venture,
Yet clumsy in their ways.
Sometimes they can't bear to face it
Another misunderstanding, another day

7. AMBITIONS

Thoughts on what it takes to achieve.

BEGINNING

A practical dreamer,
Can you be both,
Write scintillating rhymes to pass your
time
And still not burn toast?
Can you make stars
With a ladder and a chisel?
Or do you need more
Of the talents God gives you?
Leaving the material world behind
You are searching the recesses of your
mind
For all the answers to all the questions
We have begun a great journey to true
connection
With a single step:
Communicating our thoughts
With pure tenderness

DREAM MORE

If you are a writer
How can you not be a dreamer?
Take a whole world of fiction
And making something real.
It's our raison d'etre
To make characters breathe,
To bring sorrows to life,
To escape the horrors of inexpression
And hopefully delve
Into dreamworlds worth really knowing.

DISCIPLINE

Don't let your frayed garment
Dissolve completely into dust.
Repair yourself, take care of yourself
When and where you must.

THE FUTURE

Bellies overflowing;
Heart burnt and black;
Forgotten.
Television on;
Soul disconnected;
Job on the line;
Fitness in decline.
Welcome to the New World Order.
Belief is not hereditary:
It is earned through observance
And listening and trust.
Consciousness abating
Obedience a must.

FREEDOM

It's what we live for;
It's what they died for.
Chasing down shadows in haunted
trenches
We live now thanks to them.
Though bound by law and obligation
To those beside us
As we ride
Into a future as troubled as it is endless.

CEASE

The taste of medicinal drugs in the
mouth
Mingle with yesterday's dreams.
Yes, I live,
No blood spills,
That's intact
Dirt flowing through my veins.
I have been in this prison at least twenty
years
Feigning understanding
Though I have none.
At times, I must confess,
I yearn for the day when all this will
cease

MORNING

Morning comes and carves a way
Winding through another day
The afternoons are all marooned
Neither here nor there
The prime time is the nighttime
All stars and sorrow bare

FROM MY HEART

I don't care if no one listens,
I will speak my piece.
I have things to say that will shock you.
Listen, you in your judgemental haze
Judge on -
You dare to remonstrate?
Shouting "NO!" in beauty's face?
Of this I want no single part
I will speak on from my heart

DANCER IN THE DARK

Is belief part of the horror?
A refuge only to the insane -
Or something more profound:
Find the courage to engage
With the questions which are hallowed
ground to the Saints,
The ones which have no answers.
For in the dark
A violin plays,
And you, my dear, are a dancer

CHANGE

We can change the world.
Each thought,
Each act of righteousness,
Works towards a dawning bliss
Where all have provisions.
When safety and health
Are not wistful fancies,
Like angels and wealth.

HOMEWORK

I should be more competitive.
I'm happy with nothing
Except my words
And a handful of people
To while away the hours with.
Come deserts or showers
I'll always be there for you.
Not for me the rat race
Or climbing ladders to nowhere;
I always passed the tests
But I never did the homework

REVOLUTION

The revolution starts here.
Tonight.
The vision is golden,
The future is bright,
When you give your all
To what you believe in.
You connect to a force
Superior to the self,
Moving around your will and whim
The melody of life is rearranged.

A MEANINGFUL LIFE

Nothing is meaningless.
No thought, deed or sound.
All has ancient origins.
Trace the act to its source;
There lies the first domino
Falling into infinity.
No one can see it,
But it's not disconnected.
From the words I speak now
And the stirring in your heart

WISHING WELL

The battle for belief
Is the bloodiest of all:
Who on Earth can find a meaning
Through the plagues and the wars?
Saviours crucified,
The millions still searching
For the meaning of life,
Or at least a glimpse behind the curtain.
"At best a cruel lie"
Says the man at the back,
His vision impaired
Through years of abuse
Of Lady Wisdom, so fair.
The truth is not ugly:
It's beautiful and free,
Exhibited from all sources,
Prodded easily from me.
And I throw another coin
In my very own wishing well.

CLARITY

Tracks for a train;
Tracks on the arm of a drug user;
Both scream of escape.
Veins on a plant leaf;
Veins in the bodies of animals;
All crave light and love.
The howl of a lone wolf;
A love letter through the post;
Both have a place in the wild.
The uncontrollable nature of life.
With each word I speak,
Must I roll a dice
That says "misunderstanding";
On one or more sides?
I'll make myself clear one day ...
Or else I'll die.

VISIONARIES

There are clearly too many confused
people in the world:
Those without vision are just as clearly
drawn to positions of great power
While the true visionaries cower under
rocks
Tormented by their sight.

PERFECTION

I'm writing some of the best poetry I
have ever written;
I can feel it all coming to fruition.
Years of learning how to translate
Thought into word so that it takes
The reader by surprise.
See the power and the pride
Knocking on perfection's door.

ALWAYS AND FOREVER

I didn't find the strength to live my
dreams
So instead I am living a nightmare:
The could have been,
Would have been,
Should have been.
The never was.
Drowning in regret,
I suffocate in despair
At the thought of me once
Seeing you there,
The sun to my moon
The child I never had.
Oh to go back
And seize with both hands
That which is mine
Always and forever

UNTIL THE END OF ETERNITY

Holding on to the light
Will burn you.
Let it burn bright
And turn to
Another source of wisdom,
A higher source of truth,
That which you find
Deep within you.
This is the light that inflames the light
itself
Even as you watch it burn.
You know all is well
For this is all to cling to
Until the end of eternity.

CLAIRVOYANCE

I knew it was coming
Before it was so.
A death or a blessing
A vision will show
What's soon to occur
No reason, no word
Just a violent understanding of what will
potentially come to pass.
Although I can see the future
I am unable to comprehend the past.
It takes years to be at peace with
yourself
The confusion is dumbfounding.
It's like an ant of wisdom
Looking up at a mountain.
Yet rather than descend into a Hell of
my own making,
Burning like the forests around the
world,
My world has become now so cold I am
shaking
As I make footprints in the newly fallen
snow
Leading the way for others to follow.

FLOWERS

The seeds and bulbs have all been
planted
Yet the flowers have not bloomed.
Those who professed of their upcoming
beauty
Spoke too soon.
The soil has turned to dust,
All is arid.
We really must
Pray and dance for rain and things
Like the ancients taught us.
Sing!
And live in tune with all of life.
Don't be burdened by the strife:
We'll toil and sow
In rain or snow
To make sure that these flowers grow.

SPACE

What will the future hold?
Will we live to see it?
Where is the danger coming from?
Let's try hard not to be it.
Be gentle with one another
For we are all walking on a precarious
Earth
Circling smoothly,
Yet lurching wildly,
As we make our way through space

LIFT YOUR HEAD UP

"On the darkest day of the year
People are looking for light."
Even the newsreader on television
Has turned into Rumi for the night,
For poetry surrounds us
Particularly in our despair.
Whether we define it as such
Is neither here nor there.
A newborn baby's touch:
It rhymes
With the flowers in the meadow
As they caress and reach for light.
Don't you dare hold your head low

THE RECKONING

Start a revolution
Right here, right now,
And fight the court jester
Who's wearing the crown.
This world belongs to everyone,
Some rich, some poor,
If you don't let us in nicely
We'll kick in the door,
For redemption must be attained.
Equality beckons
From this hellishness refrain
Or with God be reckoned

FIVE GOLD RINGS

Having touched the stars of Heaven,
I scratch my head
And look at my compass.
I have so much to guide me,
So many people beside me,
Serenading me through the day
With good old fashioned charm.
Not that there aren't people out there
Who wish and do me harm.
I take no notice
And hold my gold
To fashion jewellery
For you to hold

THE LONG JOURNEY TO WISDOM

On a journey:
Drying up in the mouth,
Do I have enough resources
To survive let alone thrive?
I reach for some water
From you, my companion.
Some good news or cheer
To quench my thirst.
Listen, tread lightly,
The angels are near
And will reward you for your
endeavours.
There's no need to fear:
'Tis all a fiction
Written by your own hand;
Our journey to places
We don't yet understand.

A POETRY ISLAND

A poetry island
Where no one escapes,
We just rhyme and riddle
Until the end of our days
Admiring the beaches, the fishes, the
shore
All would be serenaded.
And best of all,
There would be no government.
Just you and I,
The birds in the sky,
And blank sheets of paper
Upon which to write
Our purest admirations.
The battles we've seen
All seeming now
As if within a dream.
We'd eat the coconuts
Then drum through the night
By the open fire
Squealing our delight.
At life in the very slow lane,
No racing, no fuss,
Just a long conversation
Between you and the gods.

MY SEARCHES FOR MEANING

Learning how to write takes time:
Which words are yours, which words are
mine?
A comma misplaced, a semi-colon
misused,
It's enough to make you lose sleep.
Abused
The English language runs away
screaming
But it was just silly me and my searches
for meaning.

Printed in Great Britain
by Amazon

30960015R00086